IMAGES OF ENGLAND

CHESTERFIELD
PICTURE THE PAST

T0346755

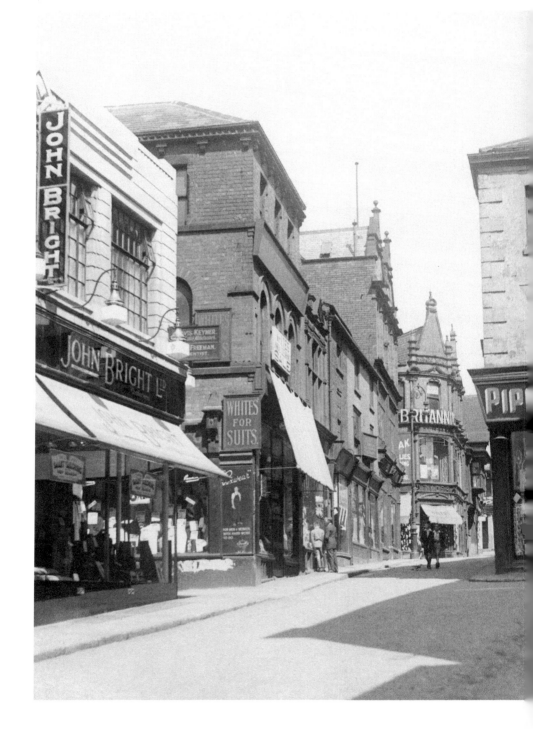

IMAGES OF ENGLAND

CHESTERFIELD
PICTURE THE PAST

ANN KRAWSZIK

Frontispiece: Looking along Packers Row in the 1930s. Church Lane is opposite the entry to The Shambles which is on the left. (DCCC001631)

First published in 2005 by Tempus Publishing

Reprinted in 2013 by
The History Press
The Mill, Brimscombe Port,
Stroud, Gloucestershire, GL5 2QG
www.thehistorypress.co.uk

British Library Cataloguing in Publication Data.
A catalogue record for this book is available from the British Library.

ISBN 978 0 7524 3581 7

Typesetting and origination by
Tempus Publishing Limited.
Printed in Great Britain.

Contents

Acknowledgements

All of the images featured in this book are in Chesterfield Library's local studies section, and have been collected over many years. Sincere thanks go to everyone who has offered photographs to the library, to those who have given permission for them to be digitised and included on the 'Picture the Past' website, and to those who allowed their images to be published in this book. Unfortunately, some photographs were given to the library so long ago that it has been impossible to contact the donors about publication. Every effort was made to trace donors.

In addition to the many individuals who donated the images of early Chesterfield which have been selected for inclusion in this book, particular thanks go to Mike Wilson, editor of the *Derbyshire Times* newspaper, for permission to include their photographs of the view of the town in 1951, the New Beetwell Street area and the old courthouse on pages 12, 18 and 76.

The image on page 76 of the slipper baths on South Place is reproduced by permission of *The Star*, Sheffield.

Mr G.W. Martin, Mr J. Phipps, Mr H. Dymond and the Chesterfield & District Photographic Society are also thanked for permission to use some of their images. Thanks go to the families of Mr R. Wilsher, Mr G. Hancock and Mr J. Cannam, who also gave permission for publication.

The work of photographers in the early 1900s should also be acknowledged. Because of Seaman, Waterhouse, Nadin and Rippon, images of Chesterfield at the turn of the twentieth century have been recorded and preserved forever.

Grateful thanks also go to Chesterfield Borough Council for permission to publish photographs commissioned by them when the town was being altered and modernised in the 1920s and '30s.

Introduction

All of the images included in this book are to be found on the website
www.picturethepast.org.uk, which forms the North East Midland Photographic Record.
The website contains over 45,000 images held in library and museum collections in
Derby, Nottingham and the counties of Derbyshire and Nottinghamshire, and new
images are added every week. The digitisation project has been made possible by a grant
of £37,000 from the Heritage Lottery Fund to produce a database with the aim of
preserving the original images and to enable them to be enjoyed by anyone anywhere
in the world with internet access. It is possible to find all of the photographs included in
this book on the site, and either print off a low-resolution copy at home on a printer, or
pay for photographic quality prints to be sent to you via an ordering system. The web
reference number for each photograph has been added at the end of each caption for
ease of identification. You can order prints online.

It has been quite a task to select photographs for this book. Hundreds are available on
Chesterfield alone, and I wanted to choose as many images as possible that had not been
published before. I also wanted to include images of the main Chesterfield buildings
and themes. What book about Chesterfield would be complete without a photograph
of the 'Crooked Spire' church or the three railway stations which once operated in
the town? Inevitably some of the images selected have been published before; there
have been many excellent books produced with photographs of Chesterfield and it is
impossible not to duplicate a few. I hope that the final selection gives a rounded view of
Chesterfield and includes a good proportion of images not previously seen.

I have had to limit this selection to Chesterfield town centre, which is a relatively
compact area, but there are a few glimpses of Derby Road, Ashgate Road and Sheffield
Road. Districts such as Hasland, Newbold, Spital and Whittington Moor have been
omitted because of the vast amount of choice available for Chesterfield itself.

The photographs show the development of the town over time. Some areas have
hardly changed at all, such as the Market Place and The Shambles, while others have

changed beyond recognition. This is why I have included the section on Beetwell Street, which has virtually been rebuilt. The photographs show a street being radically transformed, and offer a view of a once narrow street with entrances to the many yards coming off it, leading to premises on the Market Place and Low Pavement. Saltergate and Holywell Cross have also undergone major transformations and some fine buildings have been lost. Chesterfield is fortunate, however, to have retained so much of its character, as can be seen in the layout of the streets and the retention of so many old buildings.

It is my hope that by looking at and enjoying the photographs selected here from the 'Picture the Past' site, readers will be encouraged to go onto the website for themselves and see more photographs of Chesterfield (and the other places in the region covered by the project) in times gone by.

The work of the digitisation project for 'Picture the Past' continues. If anyone has photographs in their possession which they would like to see included on the site, then they are welcome to offer them to Derbyshire Library Service for inclusion.

Ann Krawszik B.ED MCLIP
Local Studies Librarian
Chesterfield Library

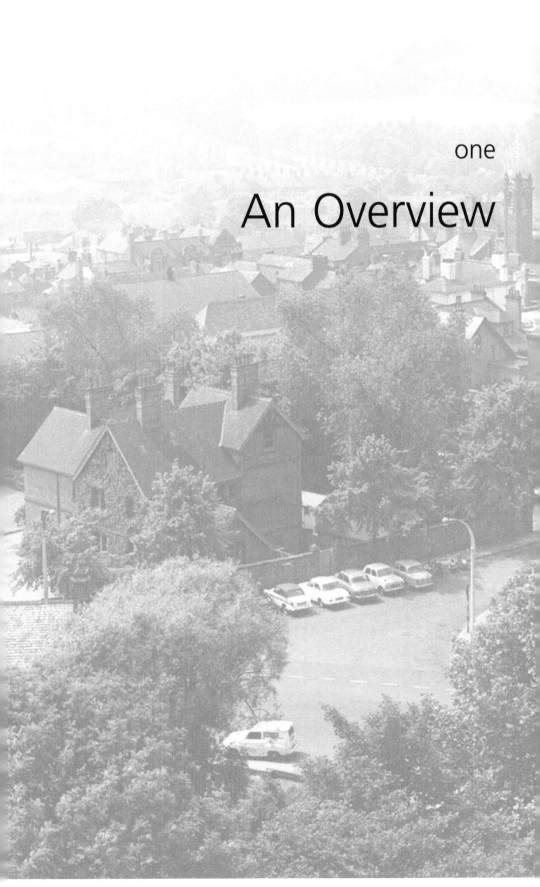

one

An Overview

A very early representation of Chesterfield, from the 1830s or earlier. The view is from Hady Hill looking towards Lordsmill Street and is taken from an oil painting. The house directly in front of the church is Mr Malkin's house, part of which remains as the *Derbyshire Times* building on Station Road. (DCCC001489)

An elegant-looking and possibly idealised Chesterfield in 1849, seen from the south–west in an image taken from a lithograph. The tall chimneys are evidence of industrial activity in the town. Several rather grand houses can also be seen, such as West House on the left with Rose Hill behind it in the trees. The tower of Holy Trinity Church is in the distance. (DCCC001496)

The town as seen from Spital Cemetery, which opened in 1857. Joseph Clayton's tannery is in the centre near the railway bridge – he was a pioneer of 'chrome tanning', the process of producing leather by treating skins with basic chromium sulfate. The Market Hall is visible. (DCCC001495)

Chesterfield in around 1890, seen from Tapton. The Midland Railway is in the foreground, with Crow Lane running under the bridge. The road sweeps round in front of the original Midland Station and the Station Hotel. The Temperance Hotel and the Midland Hotel are to the left, and on Tapton Lane near the tree is the Railway Inn. (DCCC001323)

Looking westwards over the town centre in August 1951. The Market Hall can clearly be seen facing The Shambles and the narrow Church Lane running parallel to Burlington Street. The Town Hall is in the top right-hand corner. (DCCC001417)

The southern aspect of the town from the church, looking over the Vicarage on the left to Boythorpe in 1962. Church Lane and Church Way are in the foreground, and Queen's Park is in the distance. (DCCC001447)

Chesterfield in 1962. Stephenson Place is in the foreground, and further back is the curved front of the Blue Bell public house. Holywell Street is still built up as it leads to Newbold Road. Ryland Works Ltd is in the top left-hand corner – this company supported the pipe-making industries and sold kitchen equipment, bathroom suites and heating appliances. (DCCC001449)

The Great Central Railway line, leaving the station northwards in 1962 on the route now used by the A61 inner relief road. The tall building of the college dominates. Also visible is the chapel on Brewery Street and the Odeon cinema in the foreground. (DCCC001452)

Left: Looking along High Street in 1965. The Market Hotel can be seen in the bottom left. This had previously been called the Post Office Vaults and New Square Inn. (DCCC001431)

Below: Further along High Street, this time in 1959. The shop of Samuel Hadfield & Sons (local pork butchers) can be clearly seen. Hadfield had several shops in town. The mock Tudor buildings on Knifesmithgate stand out. Knifesmithgate was in existence as early as 1385, and was probably named after a family (cf. John le Knyfsmyth) rather than literally being a street on which knives were made. (DCCC001450)

The Market Place in 1959. Greaves' chemists shop is on the corner of Tontine Road. The shops on Low Pavement (on the right) have narrow fronts, with long buildings behind enclosing the Yards. Hady Hill is in the distance. (DCCC001448)

A view of Rose Hill showing the newly built Town Hall (with the Chesterfield Rural District Council offices behind it on Saltergate) in 1938. The new road was extended from Knifesmithgate across Glumangate. The Congregational Chapel stands isolated on Soresby Street, and the Masonic hall is at the top right. (DCCC001615)

Looking over New Beetwell Street, Park Road and the railway tracks to Queen's Park and Boythorpe in 1959. (DCCC001454)

West Bars in 1959, with the Market Place Station next to the Portland Hotel. There is a clear view of the railway sheds and tracks of the Lancashire, Derbyshire & East Coast Railway (LD&ECR), and evidence of industry in the distance at Brampton. New Square is in the foreground. (DCCC001451)

The LD&ECR embankment from the south, in a photograph taken in the late 1950s. The Chesterfield Tube Company is in the foreground. (DCCC001420)

A photograph taken from the same vantage point and at the same time as the previous one, but this time looking over towards Tapton. Derby Road is clearly visible, with the Midland Railway crossing under the LD&ECR line. (DCCC001345)

The back of Low Pavement seen from Markham Road in 1973, before the redevelopment of the Yards. (DCCC001409)

In 1973 New Beetwell Street was extended so that it met West Bars, and in this photograph building work is in progress on the project. (DCCC001413)

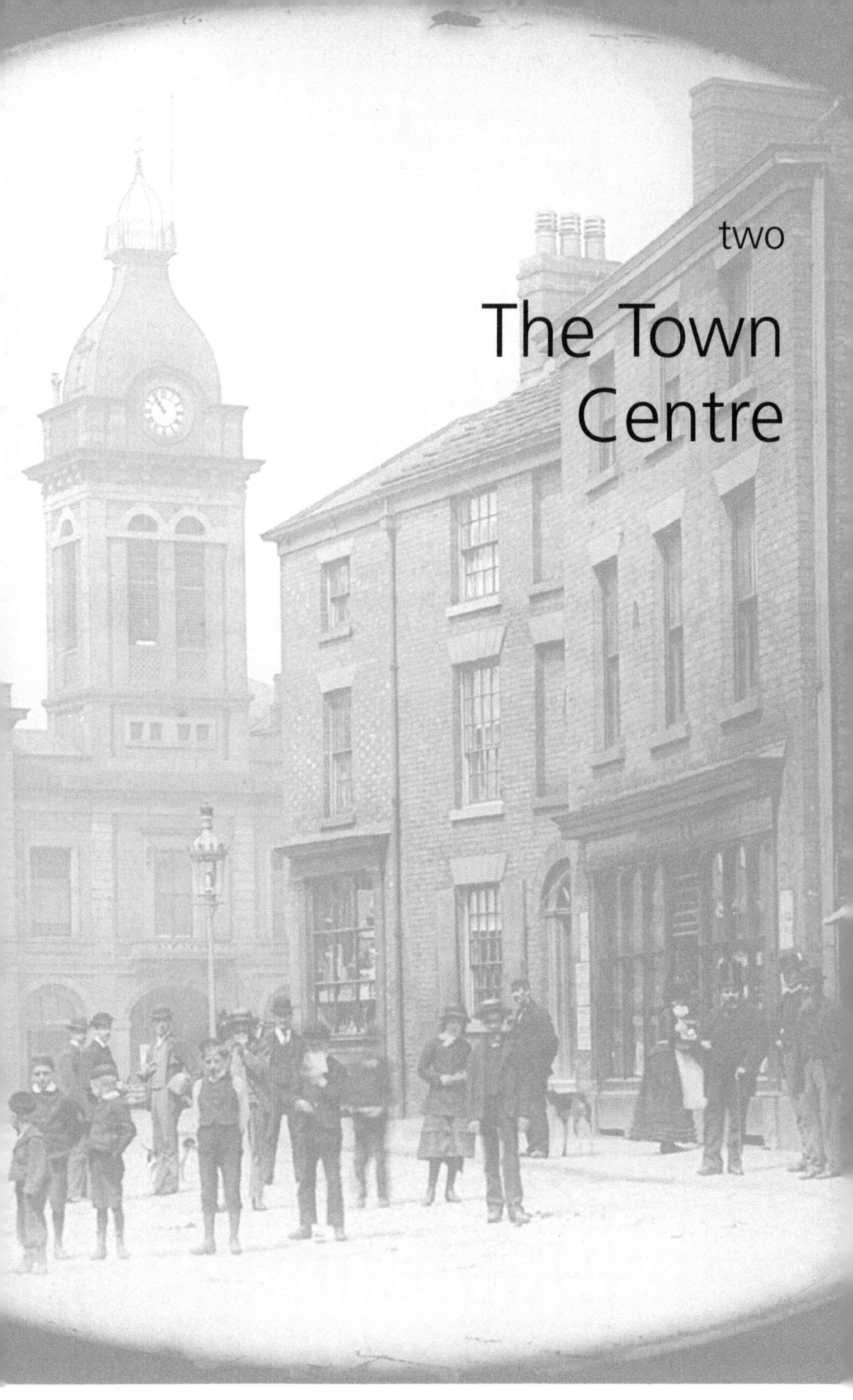

two

The Town Centre

An image of the Market Place (*c.* 1865) taken from a lithograph. Chesterfield's very first recorded Market Hall was built in 1675. The original Town Hall is on the north-west corner of the Market Place and was built in around 1790. (DCCC 001254)

The Market Place in 1890. It was used for cattle sales before the purpose-built cattle market opened on Markham Road in July 1900. At one time bull-baiting took place here to provide sport and to let people know that bull beef would be available to buy. The Star Inn can be seen up on High Street between the Angel Hotel and the bank at the corner of Glumangate. (DCCC001252)

Central Pavement in around 1900. (DCCC001532)

Looking across the canopies of the market stalls to Low Pavement in around 1910. There was no break in the shops along Low Pavement as Tontine Road was not built until 1914. Packers Row was extended at this time, and there was no easy access to Vicar Lane from Low Pavement. (DCCC000005)

Above: Three Tuns Yard in 1911. This site is now the pedestrian walkway from the Market Place to the public library and the shopping precinct and, prior to that, Tontine Road. (DCCC000038)

Left: Barker's shop on Low Pavement in 1914, on the corner of the newly built Tontine Road and the site of the Three Tuns public house and yard. Barker's was established in the 1890s and closed in the 1940s, to be replaced by Hardy's furniture shop. (DCCC001517)

Opposite, below: By 1934 W. Dutton ran the chemist shop in the corner building on the left. Tontine Road (here between Greaves' chemists and Barker's) was built to allow easy access to the cattle market. Greaves' was known for its famous tall window, built to avoid window tax. Note that Vicar Lane was accessible from Low Pavement by this time. (DCCC001627)

Above: The corner of Tontine Road and New Beetwell Street in the late 1930s. The building on the right was the police station, next to the fire station on the extreme right. (DCCC000357)

Looking up Tontine Road towards the Market Place in the 1960s. The pub called Cathedral Vaults was also known as 'Pretty Windows'. Greaves' chemists is on the left opposite Hardy's furniture shop. (DCCC001597)

The junction of Tontine Road and Markham Road in the 1960s. The entrance to the cattle market can be seen and the bus station is in the foreground. (DCCC001613)

Low Pavement in around 1900. The narrow frontages of the shops can be clearly seen here. Low Pavement was originally known as East Bars and had also been called Toll Corner and Toll Nook. (DCCC001508)

Low Pavement, looking in the opposite direction towards Packers Row in the early 1900s. There was no roadway through to Vicar Lane at this time. Turner's drapers shop was established in around 1855. The Everest Dining Rooms were in what was once the Falcon Inn, an old coaching house. (DCCC001371)

Vicar Lane in the 1960s, showing the Corporation Central Bus Station on the left. The oddly shaped roof belongs to Turner's shop and the Red Lion Inn is near to the Shell petrol sign. (DCCC001593)

New Square in the 1960s. This square used to be called Swine's Green, and then Pig Market. It dates from 1827, when the previous Market Hall was demolished, and was originally an open piece of land with a pond. The Portland Hotel and the post office building are in the centre.(DCCC001609)

Above, left: The junction of Park Road and New Square in 1973. (DCCC000578)

Above, right: This photograph was taken during the 1920s from the corner of Park Road and New Square, looking along West Bars. The building behind the billboards was the goods shed belonging to the Market Place Station, which is hidden from view on the left. Tramlines run along West Bars, and the overhead cables used by the trolleybuses are visible. (DCCC000841)

West Bars in around 1910, looking towards the market. The Portland Hotel is on the right – it took its name from the Duke of Portland, one of the many former Chesterfield Lords of the Manor. It was built on the site of the White Horse and the Bird In Hand Inn, and was opened in 1899. (DCCC000223)

The Market Place Station in a photograph taken soon after it was opened in 1897. The clock has yet to be installed. This was the third station to be opened in Chesterfield, and was built on land called Maynard's Meadows, which had been named after a local landowner and town mayor. Market Place Station was the headquarters of the Lancashire, Derbyshire & East Coast Railway, which had plans to link Warrington, Chesterfield, Lincoln and Sutton-on-Sea by rail. However, only the Chesterfield to Lincoln section was completed. The company was taken over in 1907 by the Great Central Railway. The last passenger train ran through this station in 1951, and the last freight services in 1957. It was finally demolished in 1983. (DCCC000426)

The Market Place Station in 1952. The Town Hall can be seen in the distance and the Portland Hotel is on the right. (DCCC 001465)

A peaceful-looking West Bars in 1937, looking towards the railway station. Behind the wall used to be the roller skating rink, which was opened in 1909. The rink was a large building with room for 250 skaters, and it was also used for fairs, carnivals, trade exhibitions, boxing matches and public meetings. It burned down in 1932. The notice advertises the 'Chesterfield Municipal & Derbyshire Industries Exhibition', which was held between 6 October and 16 October 1937 and was described as the 'largest exhibition ever held in Derbyshire', with 260 stands. The site today is roughly where the Shentall Gardens are, in front of the Town Hall. (DCCC001617)

Clarence Road at West Bars. The horse-drawn tram (No.7) dates the image to before 1904, when the electric tram was introduced to Chesterfield. (DCCC001486)

Construction work on the West Bars roundabout in 1963, at the point where Boythorpe Road, Chatsworth Road and the newly constructed Markham Road met. Industrial sites can be seen, with the Brampton Brewery buildings on the right. A brewery was first established here in 1839. Part of the Wheatbridge Pottery can be seen, with the Wheatbridge Mills behind. West Bars is believed to have derived its name from a gate which once stood across the road, preventing cattle from straying into the town. (DCCC001130)

Boythorpe Road seen from West Bars in the 1930s. There is a railway crossing at the narrowest point, linking the industries in the Brampton area.(DCCC000976)

Left: Wheeldon Lane (seen here from the Market Place) was one of a number of lanes and yards which ran from Low Pavement to the River Hipper. It was named after an Elizabethan family who lived near the river, and was once called Steppestone Lane. Brayshaw's printing works occupied Mason's Tobacco factory site. Today this is the site of the pedestrian footbridge from the multi-storey car park to the shopping precinct. (DCCC000917)

Below: The Dog Kennels was an area south of the Market Place which contained overcrowded houses cramped together, a place renowned for deprivation and poverty. This is Bradshaw Place off Markham Road in around 1911. The actual 'dog kennel' was between the Silk Mill and Wheeldon Lane. (DCCC000037)

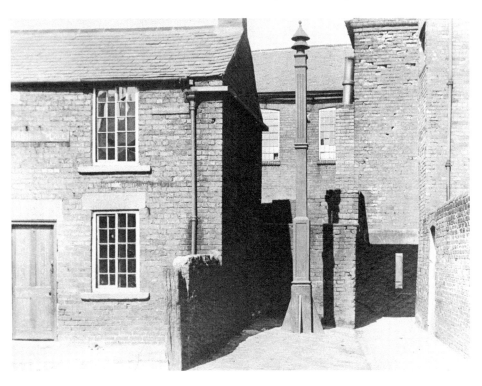

Hopkinson's Yard, another area of the Dog Kennels, in a photograph taken in 1911. There were six houses in the yard, which was in the vicinity of Lordsmill Street. Three of the houses were uninhabited by 1900 and were condemned by the sanitary inspector. The Dog Kennels were demolished in 1912 when Markham Road was built. (DCCC000001)

This photograph was taken in around 1880, looking along High Street in the days before trams. The *Derbyshire Courier* newspaper offices are on the left. High Street was once called High Pavement. (DCCC001533)

Left: High Street, sometime after 1904, looking towards the Market Hall. Electric tram tracks and overhead wires are visible. (DCCC001218)

Below: A view of High Street in around 1885. T.P. Woods' wine and spirit merchants stands out. T.P. Woods was mayor of Chesterfield three times – in 1873, 1885 and 1886. The market pump dates back to the early nineteenth century. (DCCC000310)

Above: The Shambles in 1887. The Market Place is in the distance. Note the overhanging eaves of the buildings, the narrow path and the slope of the pavement, which formed a channel. The Shambles contained the town's butchers' shops, originally called 'Flescheharnles', and then 'le Shambles' by 1560. This compact area, containing a maze of narrow pathways, maintains its medieval layout even today. Other nearby rows were called Draper Row, Fisher Row, Iron Row and Potter Row. (DCCC000921)

Left: The Shambles in the 1930s, still showing many of the same features. The Royal Oak claims to be the oldest public house in Chesterfield, and one of the oldest in England. (DCCC001563)

Opposite, below: Packers Row in 1964. There are several possible reasons for the name of this street, the most likely being that it is a corruption of 'Packhorse Row', having been originally named at a time when horses were used to transport goods. (DCCC 001432)

Above: Packers Row to the north of Burlington Street and High Street around 1900. Woodhead's coffee house is the curved building on the left. Frith's was a drapers and outfitters next to Miss Booker's restaurant and tea rooms. On Packers Row itself, on the right of the photograph, is the Flying Dutchman Inn and J. Harrison's boot and shoe shop, while on the corner is the Livingstone Café. (DCCC001632)

Packers Row in the 1930s. Woodhead's Café was part of a large business comprising several shops in the area, and had its own bakery. (DCCC001630)

High Street in 1884. J.H. Gregory had a mobile shop to take goods out to the districts. (DCCC000389)

Burlington Street in the 1930s, showing the Swallows department store. Swallows first traded in 1862. Woodhead's Café is on the right on the corner of Packers Row, on a part of High Street once called Mercer Row, and later Draper Row. Burlington Street was built in around 1837, and was originally called New Street. (DCCC001291)

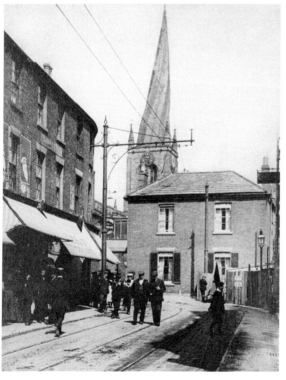

The end of Burlington Street in around 1907, before the end house was demolished to make way for the Alpine Gardens in 1908. The house belonged to a Dr Black, and then a Dr Green. Alpine Gardens was a gift to the town from Alderman T.P. Woods, but was later removed to create Church Way. (DCCC000922)

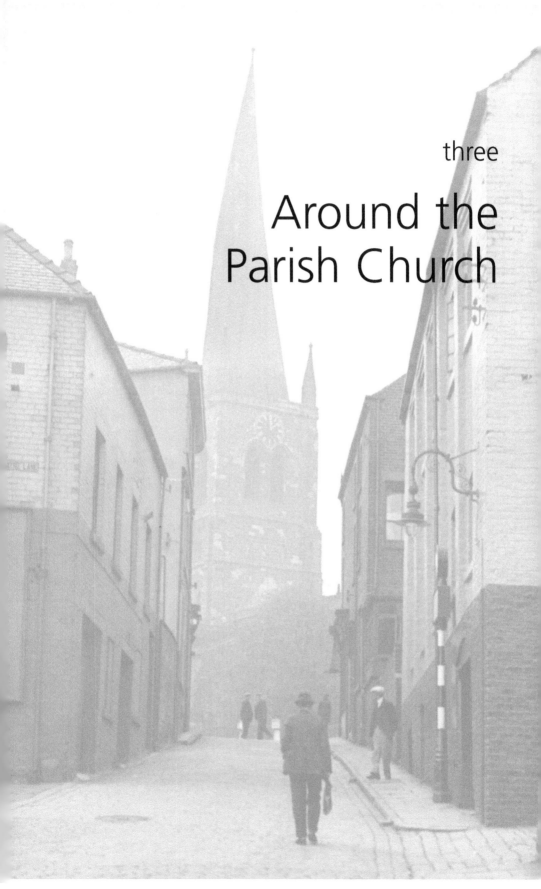

three

Around the
Parish Church

Lordsmill Street, looking towards Horns Bridge in around 1910. The street is believed to have been named because at one time it led to a corn mill on the River Hipper which was owned by the Lord of the Manor. (DCCC001537)

Lordsmill Street, again in around 1910, only this time looking back the other way towards St Mary's Gate. (DCCC001534)

St Mary's Gate in the 1960s. This view from the parish church shows the Swan Inn in the foreground and the buildings up to Heathcote's House, which is painted white. The entrance to Terra Firma Place is along here and the entrance to Elliott's Yard is next to the Swan Inn. (DCCC001640)

St Mary's Gate (c. 1900) with the Anchor Hotel on the right-hand side. To the left is Church Lane. (DCCC000010)

Above: Church Way in the late 1920s. It was originally called Church Lane. The first Crooked Spire Inn can be seen with a sign outside. (DCCC000179)

Left: These cottages on Church Alley were demolished in the 1920s when Church Lane was widened to create Church Way, on the site of what is today Rykneld Square. Church Alley used to have a chantry house on it. (DCCC001568)

Opposite, below: The parish church in around 1920. There was a church on this site in Saxon times, and it was called All Saints as late as 1793. The oldest part of the present building is from 1234, with fourteenth-century additions. The Calvary Cross war memorial was unveiled in 1919 by Sir Ernest Shentall. (DCCC001459)

A close-up of the crooked spire of the church of St Mary and All Saints. The herring-bone pattern of the lead plates emphasises the twist. The spire is octagonal, reaches 228ft above the ground and leans over 9ft from centre. The spire was built at the end of the nineteenth century and is covered with thirty-two tons of lead tiles. It became twisted because of the action of the heat of the sun on unseasoned timber. (DCCC001441)

Above: Houses on Spa Lane in 1972. There are still metal bumps (or 'scotches') in the gutter today – some can be seen here. They were to stop carts from rolling downhill. Spa Lane was named after a medicinal spring that was located there, which was originally called Peasepottage Well. (DCCC000982)

Left: Tapton Lane in the 1930s. This was once a major route through Chesterfield. The original Market Place was at the top of Tapton Lane during medieval times. (DCCC001561)

Opposite, above: Hollis Lane in the late 1970s, before the inner relief road was built. Hollis Lane may have been named after the Hollis family, who were Earls of Clare and later Dukes of Newcastle. It was also known very early on as Kalehalegate, as it was the road leading to Calow. Lordsmill Street is at the top of the hill, and the van is turning into Eyre Street with the Queens Hotel on the corner. This was a Whitbread pub, which closed in 1977. (DCCC001586)

Eyre Street in around 1970. Eyre Street has since disappeared with the building of the inner relief road. (DCCC001599)

The Midland Railway Station in around 1905. The original North Midland Railway was designed by Francis Thompson and built in 1840. It was closed in 1870 to make way for this much larger building, about 100 yards away. (DCCC001499)

Corporation Street in 1963. The small road on the right leads down to the Midland Hotel. (DCCC001430)

Station Road in 1936. No. 28 is on the extreme right, next to access to Smith's Yard. The Station Road area was noted for its high density housing full of poor families, who lived together in often squalid and unsanitary conditions. (DCCC000995)

The backs of the same houses on Station Road showing their yards, 1936. (DCCC000971)

Taken from Malkin Street, this photograph shows the junction of Brewery Street (to the left) with the chapel and Brimington Road (to the right) in the early 1960s. The wooden structure of the Great Central Railway Station is in the centre, dwarfed by the college building. The Trebor factory is on the site of the former Chesterfield Brewery, which was founded in 1850. (DCCC001595)

The Great Central Railway Station at the turn of the twentieth century. This was the second railway station to be opened in Chesterfield (in June 1892), and served the Manchester, Sheffield and Lincolnshire line. The station building was made of wood. In 1897 the station became part of the Great Central Railway Company. It closed in 1963 and was demolished in 1967; today the inner relief road follows the line of the former railway. (DCCC000330)

The Great Central Railway Station goods yard with delivery carts, *c.* 1910. (DCCC001460)

The College of Technology on Infirmary Road in 1964, with the corner of the Great Central Railway Station showing. (DCCC001428)

Brewery Street in 1977 – it was so-called because the Chesterfield Brewery was sited at the bottom of the road. It was taken over by the Mansfield Brewery in 1935. (DCCC001436)

Durrant Road in 1977 as it approaches the hospital buildings. It used to be called Back Lane. Its present name is taken from the Durrant family, owners of Durrant Hall, which is on the site of the original Royal Hospital. (DCCC001435)

four

Around
Saltergate

Holywell Street, looking towards Corporation Street in 1912. The numbers indicate the locations of the following properties: 1. The Volunteer Inn; 2. The Turf Tavern; 3. Whitworth's fruit shop; 4. Watts' butchers shop; 5. Fearclough's pawnbrokers; 6. Woodward's paper and toy shop; 7. Bowes' bread shop; 8. The Leopard Inn; 9. The home of vetinary surgeon Mr Martin, a three-storey Georgian house called North View. (DCCC001642)

Above, left: Holywell Street, showing Durrant House, *c.* 1890. This was the home and surgery of Dr John Bluett, who is standing by the ladder. It is believed that the child on the bicycle was his son. Holywell Street is one of Chesterfield's oldest streets. (DCCC001293)

Above, right: The same viewpoint along Holywell Street, this time in around 1916. The building with the bay window was shared by Glossop's solicitors firm and the Victoria Hotel. It was the site of the Bay Horse Inn, later renamed the Woolpack. Next to the Victoria Hotel is the Exchange Inn, previously called the Hospital Inn. (DCCC001538)

Holywell Cross, seen from Stephenson Place in around 1934. The Turf Tavern had only recently been demolished. Part of the Picture House, which was designed by local architect Harold Shepherd and opened in 1923, can be seen. It was bought by Rank and re-named the Odeon cinema in 1937. (DCCC001628)

Holywell Cross in the late 1960s showing more of Saltergate, including Damm's fruit and florist shop and Watt's tripe shop on the corner, in the centre of the photograph. The Shakespeare Inn is the mock Tudor building to the left. (DCCC001601)

Holywell Street, looking towards Newbold Road in the 1960s. Devonshire Street is on the right, and the old Post House is just visible. (DCCC001605)

Holywell Street at the junction of Newbold Road and Sheffield Road, *c.* 1900. The tower of Holy Trinity Church can be seen. (DCCC000070)

The same area in 1935, with a clear view up Newbold Road and Holy Trinity on the right. This church was built in 1838 on a site donated by the Duke of Devonshire. (DCCC001626)

A tram on Sheffield Road near Sunny Springs in around 1910, with St Helens Street on the right. Note the tin chapel on the left. (DCCC001365)

Cavendish Street seen from Holywell Cross, *c.* 1930. The original Blue Bell Inn is on the right. It was demolished and rebuilt in the 1930s by the Chesterfield Brewery. (DCCC000905)

The same corner again, but showing more of Saltergate. The first mention of Saltergate on record is from 1285. The name could refer to the route taken through the town by packhorses carrying salt from Cheshire, or to the occupation of the people on the street, curing the carcasses of slaughtered animals. (DCCC001053)

Clearing properties on Cavendish Street to make way for the Regal Cinema and Regal Buildings in the late 1930s. Knifesmithgate is in the distance and the building in the foreground is the Blue Bell Inn. (DCCC001620)

The street name Knifesmithgate is slightly misleading, as part of it was later renamed Stephenson Place. This is the area at the end of Burlington Street where Knifesmithgate meets Cavendish Street and Stephenson Place. The house with chain railings to the left of the tram is Dr Green's house, which was demolished to make way for the Alpine Gardens (Rykneld Square today). The date is around 1910. (DCCC001485)

Looking down Knifesmithgate from Stephenson Place with Cavendish Street on the right in the early 1930s. The buildings on the left were known as Tinley's Corner (Tinley sold shoes). There were still overhead wires for the trolley buses at this time. (DCCC001621)

Stephenson Place in the early 1900s. The Lord Nelson Inn is on the left and the buildings on the right were later demolished for road widening. (DCCC000456)

Stephenson Place, *c.* 1910. The elegant curved building is the William Deacons Bank. (DCCC000240)

The Rutland Hotel was originally on Knifesmithgate. It was demolished to allow for road widening, and that part of the road was renamed Stephenson Place in honour of George Stephenson. It was rebuilt, set further back as shown here, in around 1908. The Lord Nelson is on the left near the horse and cart. (DCCC000017)

Above: A view of J.K. Swallow's newly extended shop, seen from Knifesmithgate in the early 1930s. This junction with Packers Row used to be the site of the Flying Dutchman Inn, which had closed in 1910. Swallows was demolished in 1970. (DCCC001622)

Left: The original Elder Yard, looking towards Saltergate in the 1930s. It was known before 1800 as Ellor or Eller Yard, after the old English 'ellern' or elder tree. (DCCC001541) (DCCC001541)

Opposite, below: Elder Way in around 1935, seen from Saltergate after more clearance of buildings has taken place to make way for the new Co-operative Society department store. The entrance to the Unitarian Chapel can be seen, marked by the stone gateway on the left. The Victoria Palace was a picture hall; the building was formerly part of the engineering works of W. Oliver & Co. (DCCC001623)

Elder Way, seen from Knifesmithgate after some demolition had taken place but before the road was widened in the 1930s. The Second World War held up the development of this area and parts of it were left empty until building eventually resumed. (DCCC000699)

Knifesmithgate in the 1930s, before it was extended to Rose Hill. T.P. Woods' St George's soda water factory was built in 1899 as an extension to his business premises on High Street. (DCCC001624)

Demolition work allowing access to Clarence Road from Rose Hill in around 1936, in preparation for the building of the Town Hall. The Town Hall was opened in 1938 by the Duchess of Devonshire. (DCCC001273)

Holywell Cross in 1935, showing The Blue Bell Inn at the corner of Cavendish Street and Saltergate. (DCCC001618)

A view of Saltergate from 1910, with the Shakespeare Inn on the right. The tree in the distance is level with the almshouses. There was once a flour mill at the back of the almshouses. (DCCC001372)

A photograph of Saltergate from the 1970s, at the point where it joins Holywell Cross. The Shakespeare Inn and all the buildings next to it were later demolished and the site is now a car park. (DCCC001598)

Further along Saltergate in the 1930s, the entrance to the almshouses (which were built in 1875) can be seen on the left. Nearby is the entrance to Bedlam Yard, which was named after the noise of the weaving sheds which were once there. (DCCC001315)

Properties on Glumangate, possibly in the 1930s. Glumangate could mean the 'street of minstrels' (from the old English 'gleeman', meaning minstrel). (DCCC001643)

Looking down Broad Pavement from Saltergate to Knifesmithgate in the mid-1930s. Until the mid-nineteenth century this was known as Narrow Lane. (DCCC000844)

A photograph of Saltergate taken from Glumangate in 1956. The public house on the corner was once the Corner House Hotel, the Miners Arms and later the Fountain Inn. The narrow walkway is Union Walk, and the tower of Holy Trinity Church can be seen in the distance.(DCCC001526)

Left: Housing on the north side of Saltergate in the early 1900s. The archway led to a wood yard, which was marked as a 'steam saw and planing mills' on an 1878 map. This building is now No. 81 Saltergate (next to the County Hotel), and was once used as a dentist's surgery by J.W. Slack. (DCCC001587)

Opposite, above: Shepley's Yard (off Saltergate), looking through to Knifesmithgate in around 1905. This yard is probably named after William Shepley, who was a plumber and had his business here. (DCCC001097)

Opposite, below: W. Burkitt's malthouse on Soresby Street in the early 1960s, shortly before demolition. Burkitt was a corn and seed merchant. (DCCC001641)

The fronts of Nos 14 and 16 Soresby Street (on the left and right respectively) before demolition in 1938. (DCCC001195)

The backs of Nos 14 and 16 Soresby Street (from right to left) on the same day. (DCCC001196)

Saltergate near Tennyson Avenue, *c.* 1910. The big house was known as Avenue House at this time, when it was the home and surgery of Dr Edmunds. (DCCC000018)

Saltergate seen from Goldwell Hill during the 1930s. The Central School can be seen in the distance, with the wall with alternately coloured brickwork. Fairfield Road is on the left. (DCCC001307)

West Street in the early 1900s, looking towards Cross Street. (DCCC000236)

Ashgate Road at the turn of the twentieth century. This is one of J.H. Gregory's mobile shops, which he sent out from High Street. (DCCC000233)

five

Gone Forever

A view along Lordsmill Street (*c.* 1910). The shops near the hotel belong to a grocer and a confectioner. In the distance is a footbridge over the railway. (DCCC000444)

The original St Augustine's Church on Derby Road in around 1910. A replacement church was built in 1930.(DCCC001379)

The Horns Hotel on Lordsmill Street (seen here in the early 1900s) was known to have existed in the eighteenth century. It was rebuilt several times and extensively altered over the years. It was finally demolished to make way for the inner relief road in the 1980s. (DCCC001555)

Chesterfield's three railways at Horn's Bridge in around 1910; the Lancashire, Derbyshire & East Coast railway is on the highest level, the Midland line is in the middle and the Great Central line is underneath. (DCCC001384)

Horn's Bridge in the 1970s, showing a glimpse of the Horn's Hotel (with the striped brick effect). The whole area has been redeveloped now. Horn's Bridge was named after a local family. (DCCC001611)

An old cottage on the corner of Lordsmill Street and Markham Road, demolished in the 1960s. (DCCC001543)

The parish hall of St James on Vicar Lane, seen here in around 1910. Built in 1896 and presented to the parish by Revd Cecil Littleton in memory of his mother, this became known as Jimmy's and was a popular social meeting place. (DCCC001502)

The original Beetwell Hall in the 1880s. The small cottage dates from Tudor times. (DCCC001614)

The old courthouse in 1973, when it was used as a place of worship. This was previously the Municipal Hall, on the site of the old hall on Beetwell Street. It was built in 1849 after the Municipal Reform Act of 1835 and was a council chamber and police court. It played a pivotal role during the Baron de Camin riots of 1862, when the baron's anti-catholic speech in the Market Place incensed Irish residents and he had to take refuge inside the hall. (DCCC001414)

The Slipper Baths on South Street in 1980, the year in which it closed down. The baths were built in 1904 and were very busy, with an average of 210 bathers a week in 1950. Its use declined though, and it was eventually demolished in 2004. (DCCC001397)

'The Poor House' on South Place, seen here in the 1950s. It was built in the 1760s and was the home of the workhouse master. It was situated next to the first workhouse run by the Corporation. (DCCC000419)

Harrison's shoe factory from Hipper Vale in 1964. Harrison's was in the former Silk Mill, which was built in 1734 with a huge water wheel turned by the River Hipper. Silk-throwing continued there until about 1876, at which time the mill was run by the Tucker family. It was used for a variety of purposes until Harrison's boot and shoe factory moved into the premises in 1910 and it was demolished in 1967. (DCCC001426)

Above: The Scarsdale and High Peak Bank on the corner of Glumangate and High Street, in around 1890. The Star Hotel is on the left. (DCCC001576)

Right: The White Horse Inn (*c.* 1890). This inn was known to have existed as early as the 1780s. In the 1830s there was a steam corn mill in the White Horse yard. The Portland Hotel was built on this site in the late 1890s. (DCCC000850)

Opposite, above: The Corporation slaughterhouse on Markham Road in 1923. (DCCC001103)

Opposite, below: The old police station, situated at the junction of Chatsworth Road and Old Road. It was built in the 1890s as a private residence and was occupied by the postmaster of New Brampton, also serving as a post office. Later it became a doctor's surgery. It was sold to the Corporation sometime before 1914, and it was used as a police station until about 1930. It was demolished in 1971. The building next to it was a fire station. The site was originally a pinfold for stray animals. (DCCC001521)

Above: Park Hotel (formerly Park House) on West Bars; today this site is the location of Shentall Gardens, in front of the Town Hall. The Maynard family lived here – Edmund Maynard was mayor of Chesterfield in 1839, 1846 and 1851, and he owned some of the land used in 1887 to make Queen's Park. Lady Baden Powell lived at Park House as a child. (DCCC001378)

Left: The Accountant General's Department of the Post Office in 1964. A sculpture by Barbara Hepworth entitled 'Rosewall' is situated in front of the building. The AGD building was eventually demolished and the business moved onto other premises on Boythorpe Road.(DCCC001433)

Opposite, above: Tramlines being laid down on High Street in 1904. The line ran from Chatsworth Road through the town and out along Sheffield Road to Whittington Moor. Local trams were replaced by trolleybuses in 1927. (DCCC000006)

Opposite, below: Rose Hill House, which stood on the site of the Town Hall, in around 1930. It had been the home of Alderman John Brown, once mayor of Chesterfield. It was the first brick house in the town, having been built by the Thornhill family in 1730. The house was demolished in 1936. (DCCC001527)

One of Chesterfield's new trams, out on a trial run in 1904. (DCCC001226)

A gathering outside the Commercial Hotel in around 1915. This hotel was on the corner of Vicar Lane and South Street and was altered many times. The original Commercial Inn was built in the late eighteenth century by Joseph Storrs and was a coach house with stables and a blacksmith's shop, as well as a post house and meeting place for the proprietors of the Chesterfield Canal. It was demolished in 1970. (DCCC001463)

The Vicarage which stood near the church of St Mary and All Saints, photographed in around 1910. (DCCC001374)

Holywell Cross post office, on the corner of Cavendish Street and Holywell Street, during the 1890s. Also shown is J.H. Glossop's grocery shop and livery stables. (DCCC001513)

The Devonshire Arms public house stood on Holywell Street, opposite the entrance to the Royal Hospital. In the late eighteenth century it was an inn noted for its stabling, with warehouses to the rear used for goods which would be distributed using the Chesterfield Canal. The building was demolished in 1960. (DCCC001550)

The Chesterfield School Board was established in 1871 and three new schools were built soon after. This was the Durrant Road school, attended by 150 girls and 148 infants, at the turn of the twentieth century.(DCCC001520)

Almshouses on Infirmary Road, called the 'Eventide Homes'. They were built in 1907 by E. Eastwood for eight older women living on small incomes. (DCCC000674)

Opposite below: The Hipperdrome on Corporation Street in 1960. Originally called the Theatre Royal, it was built in 1896 and became the Hipperdrome in 1912. During its most successful years there were two nightly variety shows and, from around 1908, film shows. Max Bygraves and Gracie Fields performed there in the late 1940s, but it closed in 1955. (DCCC001429)

The Chesterfield to Stockwith Canal at Lockoford Lane during the 1880s. This was the original terminal basin at the bottom of Wharf Lane. At one time this was a hive of activity, with barges pulled by horses and wagons being loaded and unloaded. The canal network declined with the spread of the railways. (DCCC001507)

The demolition of Miss Booker's restaurant in the late 1920s. This property was on Knifesmithgate opposite Packers Row, with Elder Yard off to the left. In its day, Booker's was the premier dining experience in Chesterfield. Fletcher's childrenswear shop can be seen on the right. (DCCC001498)

The Friends Meeting House on Saltergate in the 1960s, which had been built in 1673 and was improved in 1770. (DCCC000671)

Old houses on Saltergate were pulled down to make way for the creation of Elder Way during the 1930s. The corner of the Central Methodist Chapel is just in view on the right. (DCCC000919)

The almshouses on Saltergate at the turn of the twentieth century. These were provided by local benefactors for eleven women described as 'poor persons of good character'. The houses were demolished in 1971 to make way for a car park. (DCCC000568)

The building with the steps is the Staffordshire Farmers agricultural suppliers, on the corner of Broad Pavement and Saltergate in 1963. The house at the end still survives. (DCCC001427)

The Chesterfield Union Industrial School on Ashgate Road in around 1900. The school was built in the early 1880s to house destitute children from the nearby workhouse. In the 1940s it became a residential home for the elderly, and was demolished in 1956. Ashgate Croft school is now on the site. (DCCC001377)

The junction of Glumangate and Saltergate during the 1890s. The man with rolled-up sleeves is Joseph Gascoyne, standing outside Gascoyne's newsagents. The Miners Arms is next door. This property was rebuilt as the Corner House by the Scarsdale Brewery Company in 1923. (DCCC001535)

The infirmary on Newbold Road (seen here in around 1910) was later to become Scarsdale Hospital. (DCCC000673)

The Chesterfield Union Workhouse on Newbold Road in the early 1900s. The workhouse closed in 192 and became part of Scarsdale Hospital. It has recently been converted into smart town houses and apartm (DCCC000327)

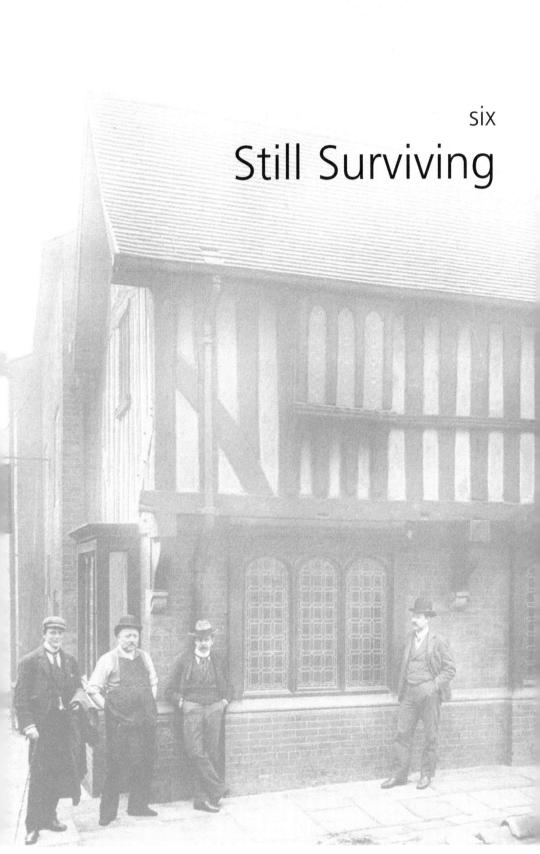

six

Still Surviving

The Bowling Green on New Beetwell Street in around 1910. This green probably dates back to the thirteenth century; it was known to exist in 1392, when it was made a gift to the Guild of Aldermen, Brethren and Sisters of the Virgin Mary and Holy Cross, and is notable for having been a bowling green continuously since that time. It was taken over by the Foljambe family in the sixteenth century, and was eventually bought by the Chesterfield Corporation. (DCCC001548)

Queen's Park in around 1910. The park was purchased by public subscription to celebrate Queen Victoria's Golden Jubilee, opening in 1887. The first county cricket match on this ground was played in 1898. (DCCC001497)

Left: Scarsdale Vaults on St Mary's Gate in the early twentieth century. The Scarsdale Brewery made ale from about 1800, and its main office (which adjoins this building) was a fine Georgian house, which still exists today. The Vaults had a number of cupolas to admit light through the roof. (DCCC000891)

Below: The Royal Hospital in the mid-1880s. It was built in 1859 on the site of the Duke of Devonshire's Durrant Hall Estate, and opened in 1860. The wards were named after benefactors such as the Markham family. The Devonshire Ward was added on in 1873 and later a nurses home was added. (DCCC001003)

Chesterfield Grammar School in around 1900. In 1598 a charter endorsed by Queen Elizabeth I established a free grammar school in an old chantry chapel of St Helen's Church. Over the centuries various students acquired eminence, notably Thomas Secker (who was Archbishop of Canterbury for ten years from 1758) and the scientist Erasmus Darwin (1731–1802).(DCCC000329)

The Stephenson Memorial Hall at the top of Corporation Street in the 1930s. Built by public subscription in 1877, it was opened by the Duke of Devonshire in 1879. It held a public hall, rooms for the Institute of Mining, Civil and Mechanical Engineers, a laboratory, public library, reading room and lecture hall. In 1889 it was sold to the Corporation. The assembly room was transformed into a theatre in 1896, and reopened in 1904 as the Corporation Theatre after electric lighting had been installed. In 1949 it was refurbished and reopened as the Civic Theatre. (DCCC001475)

No.2 St Mary's Gate in a derelict state in 1991. The oldest part was built in the early fifteenth century and was home to the Heathcote family, who were prominent in the town from medieval times onwards. Colonel Caleb Heathcote became mayor of New York at the same time as his brother Sir Gilbert was Lord Mayor of London in 1711. (DCCC001504)

The Peacock Inn on Low Pavement in 1974. It was probably originally built at the turn of the sixteenth century as a guildhall and has been much altered, with many changes of use. It was a public house by the early nineteenth century and then throughout most of the twentieth century, before becoming the town's Tourist Information Centre until 2002. It is now a coffee shop. (DCCC001439)

The Unitarian Chapel on Elder Way in around 1905. This was the first dissenting place of worship in Chesterfield and was built in 1694, paid for by eminent Presbyterian Cornelius Clarke, who was a great benefactor to the town. (DCCC001500)

A fine Georgian house on West Bars, today the business premises of a firm of solicitors, in the 1960s. (DCCC001503)

The Baptist Chapel on Brewery Street. This was the first permanent Baptist chapel, built in 1862 by voluntary contributions and opened in 1863. Beneath the chapel were schoolrooms for boys and girls. In 1927 it became part of the Royal Hospital, and Methodist worshippers moved to their new chapel on Cross Street. (DCCC001545)

Chesterfield's Ragged School, seen in the 1970s. This building has had a variety of functions over the years, including industrial uses and as a lodging house. It was turned into a Sunday school in 1878, and over 100 poor children attended. The following year it became part of the Sunday School Union. By 1885 there were 340 pupils and twenty-seven teachers. (DCCC001589)

The Sheffield Banking Company, next to the Secker's house in New Square. Thomas Secker lived here in around 1700 before becoming Archbishop of Canterbury. (DCCC001368)

The Central Methodist Chapel on Saltergate in the early twentieth century. The present church was built in 1870 to replace an earlier building, which dated from 1795. (DCCC001349)

The Roman Catholic Church of the Annunciation on Spencer Street, in around 1905. It was built between 1854 and 1874, with later alterations. The church has a stained glass window, which was placed in 1892 in memory of Mrs Lucas of Hasland Hall. Spencer is the name of a member of the Cavendish family. (DCCC001364)

Soresby Street Congregational Chapel, seen at the turn of the twentieth century. This was built on land owned by Joshua Jebb of Tapton in 1822 and was opened in 1823 to accommodate a growing Independent congregation. Revd Howard Shergold was minister at the time this photograph was taken. A Sunday school was built on nearby Marsden Street in 1860. (DCCC001362)

Holy Trinity Church on Newbold Road in around 1900. This church is famous as being the burial place of George Stephenson, the railway pioneer. (DCCC001360)

A fine row of Georgian houses on Saltergate during the 1910s. They are made entirely of brick, with all the classical architectural features of that time. (DCCC000306)

The Royal Oak in The Shambles, *c.* 1900. Built on the site of the original medieval building, this is believed to have been a rest home for crusading Knights Templar. It has had a variety of uses, and has been altered and renovated, but is known to have been an inn in 1722 (DCCC000677)

Corporation Street at the end of the nineteenth century, showing the Civic Theatre and the Stephenson Memorial Hall, after alterations had been made by the Corporation. (DCCC000893)

The Derbyshire Miners Association offices on Saltergate in around 1900, before the statues of local MPs Haslam and Harvey were erected. They were both involved with the founding of the Association. The street on the right is Clarence Road. (DCCC000676)

The offices of the Board of Guardians for the workhouse on Newbold Road in around 1900. The building was opened in 1895. (DCCC000857)

The Old Post House on Holywell Street in the late 1960s. It may originally have been a fifteenth-century yeoman's house, and has been in turn a family home, a butcher's shop, a laundry and a post office. (DCCC001583)

The Market Hotel in New Square in 1950. It shows the last example in Chesterfield of Georgian double bow windows, which date back to the 1820s. Wilfred Barker was the licensee at this time. (DCCC000651)

Compton Street was a typical street in this area of Chesterfield during the early twentieth century. The houses have names such as Raglan Villas and Ash Mount. Teachers, office clerks and employers lived in this type of house. The street is named after a member of the Cavendish family. (DCCC000243)

The Market Hall in 1937. This Market Hall was opened in 1857 by the Chesterfield Market Co., who had acquired the rights from the Duke of Devonshire. It was bought in 1874 by the Chesterfield Corporation and housed a corn exchange, butter market and assembly rooms. It is built from local brick, and the clock was a gift from the Duke of Devonshire. The hall was completely refurbished in 1979. (DCCC001255)

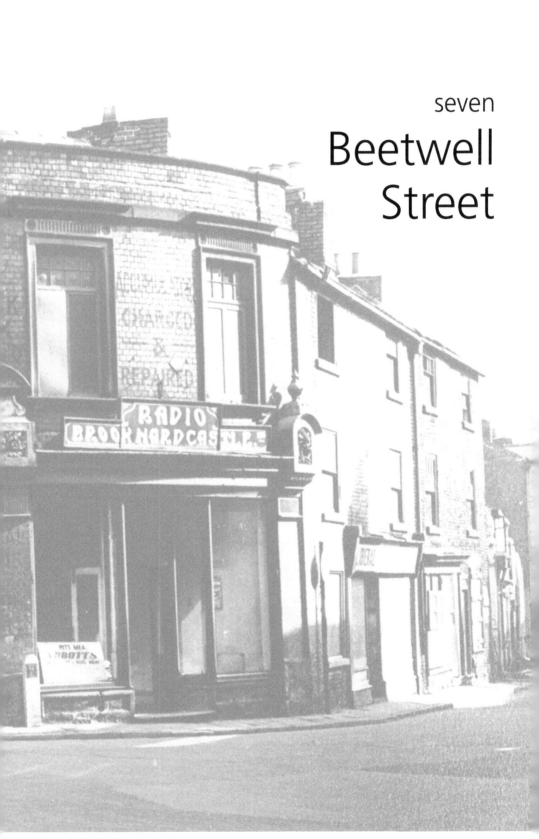

seven

Beetwell
Street

Beetwell Street seen from Lordsmill Street and St Mary's Gate in the 1930s. The origin of the street name Beetwell is unclear. It probably comes from the name of a family, or from the name of an instrument used in brewing. The street has been recorded as Betwil Lane, Stead Lane and also Market Stead Lane. (DCCC001539)

The same view in reverse. The street on the right is Hipper Street South and the Prince of Wales public house is on the left. (DCCC000812)

A view from a similar spot, this time later in the 1930s. The demolition of the buildings on the corner opened up a view to the main road. (DCCC000800)

Beetwell Street in the mid-1960s. The Prince of Wales, seen here on the right, closed in 1965. (DCCC001636)

Above: Beetwell Street, looking towards Lordsmill Street in the late 1930s. The entrance to Barrack's Yard is on the left next to Parton's shoe shop. The buildings on the right can still be seen today. (DCCC000810)

Left: This is the same row of buildings as above photographed in 1964, showing the shoe shop from a different angle. The entrance to Barrack's Yard is in the gap between the houses. Note the stone and pantile roof of the building in the foreground. (DCCC001635)

Jutting out at the end of Beetwell Street is the Municipal Hall, which was used as a courthouse in the 1930s. South Street is to the right and South Place to the left. Beetwell Street was extended in the late 1920s by the removal of the old police station. (DCCC000215)

Beetwell Street in the late 1930s, with the courthouse on the right. The tall building on the left is the fire station. (DCCC000808)

On the corner of Beetwell Street and South Street in the late 1950s was a Georgian-style quadrant building with three ornate features, which looked rather like grandfather clocks. (DCCC000187)

Beetwell Street in 1965. The buildings on the north side of the road have been demolished for road widening. There were butchers, pawnbrokers, watch repairers, fishmongers, hairdressers and tobacconists along here. Quite a few buildings survive on the south side, including the Spread Eagle, which dates back to 1479 and was at one time a coaching inn. (DCCC001438)

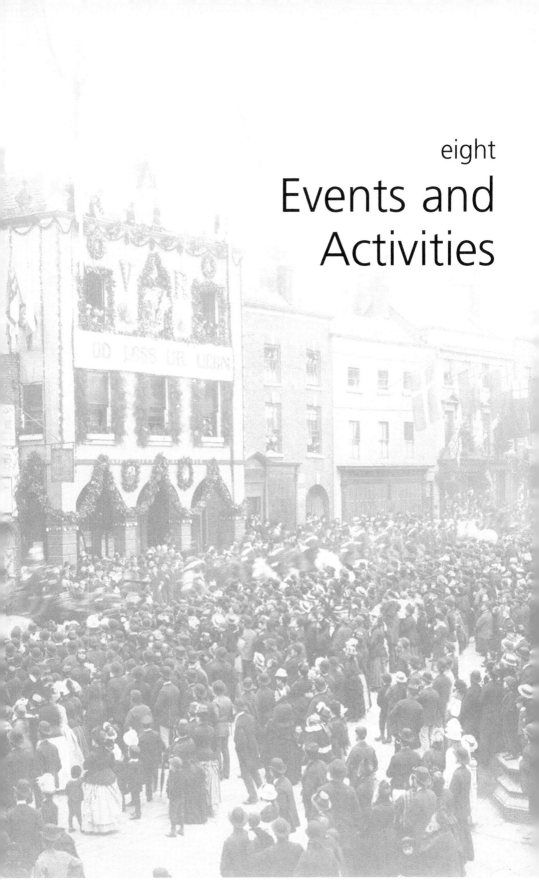

The funeral of five children, victims of the Picture Palace fire in January 1912, took place at the parish church. The tragedy unfolded when a child's costume caught fire in a changing room at the theatre, with other children catching alight in the ensuing panic. The service was led by Archdeacon Crosse. (DCCC001462)

Picking coal from spoil heaps in Brockwell during the miners strike of 1912. (DCCC001328)

On 22 December 1961 an electrical fault in the Schnetzler organ caused a terrible fire at the parish church, resulting in £35,000 worth of damage to the fabric of the building. Fifty firemen struggled for over three hours to extinguish the blaze. (DCCC001556)

Floods on Derby Road in 1958. The River Hipper has a tendency to flood and this area has been underwater many times. The Alma public house stands in isolation. (DCCC001421)

The aftermath of a riot following a railway strike on 19 August 1911, when the staff at the Midland Railway Station had to barricade themselves in. The Riot Act was read by the mayor, and there were baton charges by the police and bayonet charges by the army. (DCCC000312)

Suffragettes in the Market Place in around 1910. (DCCC001546)

The funeral of James Haslam MP in August 1913. The procession is on Corporation Street. (DCCC001330)

Swimming sports at Walton Dam in 1914. The Chesterfield Swimming Club normally used the enclosed swimming baths at the Central School, but they also held a popular annual water carnival and sports day here. (DCCC001547)

Gypsy caravans parked in the yard of the Bold Rodney public house at Brampton in the early 1920s. To the right is the Zion church, built on the site of the horse tram sheds in 1904. The houses in the background are in Alma Street. This is the site of the 'Brampton Feast', which took place in either July or August. There was a fairground with stalls and rides. The 'Brampton Feast' was a big holiday event for local people, but it came to an end in the 1950s. (DCCC001305)

An agricultural show on the recreation ground at Saltergate in around 1910. This was an annual event held at the football ground between 1887 and 1913, when it was transferred to Queen's Park. (DCCC001359)

Elephants on Chatsworth Road, part of Barnum and Baily's Circus parading through the town to advertise the show at the turn of the twentieth century. The circus was described in the *Derbyshire Times* in 1899 as 'a stupendous spectacle of men, women, children, horses, elephants, wild beasts, chariots, cars and floats'. (DCCC001391)

The cattle market on Markham Road in around 1910. Prior to 1900, cattle were sold in Chesterfield's central Market Place. (DCCC000904)

Coronation festivities off Hollis Lane in June 1911, near Markham & Co. Ltd. The gigantic 140-ton cantilever crane was made in Germany and was erected at the Broad Oaks works in 1906, and finally removed in the 1950s. It was 135ft high with a span of over 250ft and was the largest electric crane in the country at the time. Markham's has a worldwide reputation for its mechanical engineering. (DCCC001332)

At the races, near the grandstand and finishing line in the 1920s. The original stand was built in the 1830s. This one was demolished in 1928. (DCCC001494)

Right: Cleaning the course after the races in 1942. This shows the width of the course cutting a swaith through the Whittington Moor area. (DCCC001492)

Below: At the racecourse in the early 1900s. The people are looking at Proctor's bioscope sideshow, which was a forerunner of the picture house. (DCCC001571)

A more general view of the racecourse in the 1920s. Annual race meetings began in 1685, and are believed to have been instigated by the first Duke of Devonshire. Racedays were a huge public attraction. By 1836 the race meetings lasted over two days. The races ended in 1924, and houses were built on the course with street names reminiscent of the sport, such as Racecourse Road and Stand Road. (DCCC001491)

The Chesterfield Sunday School Union demonstration of witness on Whit Monday in around 1907, on Foljambe Road. (DCCC001356)

Chesterfield's Ragged School children in procession as part of a Sunday school demonstration in around 1910 on St Mary's Gate. Afterwards the children would be treated to a social event such as a party, with food and treats on offer. (DCCC001458)

The Sunday school demonstration in the Market Place, on Whit Monday in 1911. (DCCC001357)

A public gathering, possibly a miners gala at the turn of the twentieth century, taking place along Low Pavement and the Market Place. (DCCC001549)

The annual miners gala in the Market Place in May 1902. The banners from the various nearby pits are proudly on display. (DCCC000680)

The Market Place in 1901. Crowds watch the trial of a new steam-powered fire engine. The engine was built by Shand, Mason & Co. of London, and was bought by the Corporation after a destructive fire at the Ryland works had shown the inadequacy of the existing manual equipment. (DCCC001484)

Celebrations in the Market Place for Queen Victoria's Jubilee in 1887. Crowds of people have gathered to watch the procession. (DCCC000318)

The mayor of Chesterfield reading the public proclamation of the death of Queen Victoria and the accession of King Edward VII in January 1901. (DCCC001551)

Workers at J.B. White & Sons (the wine and spirit merchants) in 1894. They also had a shop on Burlington Street. (DCCC001554)

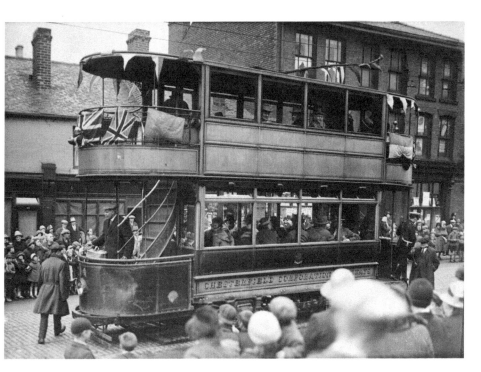

The last run of the electric tramcar in Chesterfield, on 23 May 1927. The driver is Harry Longden. (DCCC001570)

Mounted police on parade outside the police station on Beetwell Street in around 1915. Mr Kilpatrick, the chief constable, is on the white horse. (DCCC001232)

The 2nd Battalion Volunteers (Nottinghamshire/Derbyshire) procession on Saltergate in around 1910. (DCCC001560)

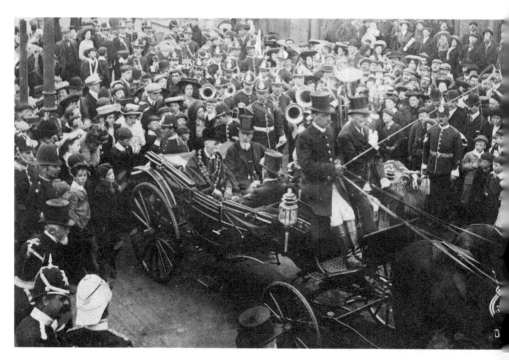

A visit by the Duke of Devonshire brought out the crowds in 1910. (DCCC001383)

A demonstration of civic pride in celebrating the tenure of Mayor T.P. Woods in 1885, at West Bars. He was born in Boythorpe in 1840, was elected to the town council at the age of twenty-three, was mayor three times and was made a Freeman of the Borough in 1887. (DCCC000019)

Mayor's Sunday in November 1911. At this time the mayor was the Duke of Devonshire. The ceremony involved a procession of civic dignitaries and the military through the town to the parish church for a service to celebrate a new mayor in post. (DCCC001512)

Other local titles published by The History Press

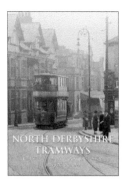

North Derbyshire Tramways
BARRY M. MARSDEN

In the heyday of trams, no fewer than seven systems operated in Derbyshire, including horse-drawn, cable and electric systems. *North Derbyshire Tramways* provides a pictorial history of trams in Chesterfield, Matlock and Glossop and includes many previously unpublished images of the towns and their public transport.

0 7524 2398 3

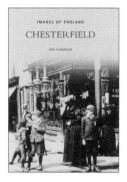

Chesterfield
ROY THOMPSON

This collection of archive photographs and accompanying captions offers a portrait of the Borough of Chesterfield in the first half of the twentieth century, before 'progress' increased the pace of life in the area. Half the book is dedicated to the old town itself; the other sections include pictures of people, industries, shops and other commercial activities which have long since passed into memory.

0 7524 3015 7

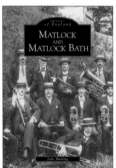

Matlock and Matlock Bath
JULIE BUNTING

This collection of archive images shows some of the diverse changes that have taken place in this area of the Peak District during the last century. The reader is given a glimpse of developments which have taken place in transport and industry; the shops and streets, and experiences of external events such as the world wars which have helped shape the nature of Matlock and Matlock Bath.

0 7524 2455 6

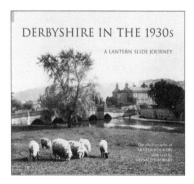

Derbyshire in the 1930s
A Lantern Slide Journey
DONALD ROOKSBY

This book takes the reader through some of the most scenic parts of Derbyshire as they looked in the mid-1930s. Pastoral scenes follow views of towns and villages, and the county town itself, all looking quieter and calmer in those pre-war days. The photographs were all taken originally to be used as lantern slides to entertain audiences in village halls around the county.

0 7524 3258 3

If you are interested in purchasing other books published by The History Press, or in case you have difficulty finding any of our books in your local bookshop, you can also place orders directly through our website
www.thehistorypress.co.uk